THE BLACK DEATH

THE PLAGUE PANDEMIC

Book Series Information:

Pandemic History - Book 2

Copyright © 2020 by **History House**.

All rights reserved.

YOUR FREE EBOOKS FROM HISTORY HOUSE!

Hello Dear History Readers!

I'm Alexander MacDonald and I created History House.

As a way of saying **Thank You** for reading our book series from History House, we're offering you a free e-Book copy every **weekend!**

Happy Reading ☺

>> Click Here <<

>> To Get Your FREE eBook <<

OTHER BOOKS BY HISTORY HOUSE:

The Spanish Flu of 1918 The Story of a Forgotten Pandemic

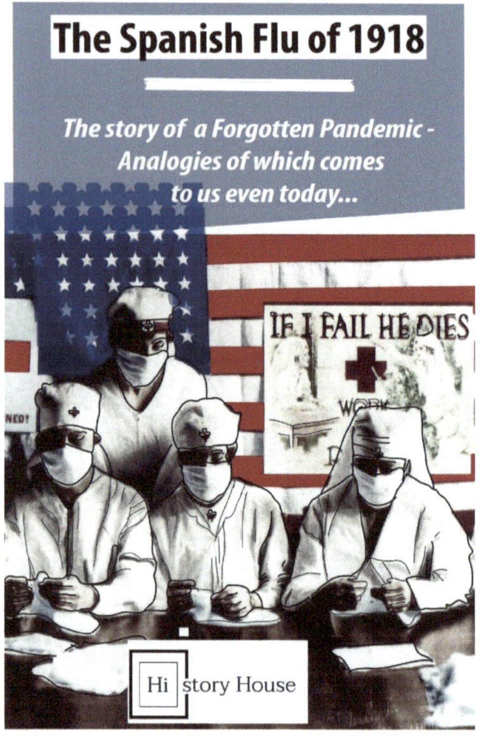

US Kindle, UK Kindle, CA Kindle, AU Kindle
* Available on all kindle markets

The Life of Anne Frank Fascinate Journey from the early years to an end

US Kindle, UK Kindle, CA Kindle, AU Kindle * Available on all kindle markets

The Life of Sir Winston Churchill Fascinate Journey - From The Early Years to an End

US Kindle, UK Kindle, CA Kindle, AU Kindle * Available
on all kindle markets

The Life of Albert Einstein: Fascinate Journey - From the early years to an end

US Kindle, UK Kindle, CA Kindle, AU Kindle * Available
on all kindle markets

INTRODUCTION

In the wake of human civilization, world pandemics rose and struck the human population in great numbers. A disease would turn into a pandemic when the infectious disease spreads across borders. The world through ages has seen outbreaks that ravaged humanity, at other times, almost alienating the whole existence of the human and animal population. And even when humans in the past didn't understand the science behind such pandemics, at times, it signaled an end of an entire civilization, flipping the course of history in less than a decade. From the earliest pandemic recorded in 430 B.C: Athens, through 11th-century leprosy pandemic, the Columbian exchange to the modern pandemic of Spanish Flu in the 1800s and COVID 19, the world has faced a substantial human causality.

The Black Death pandemic struck in the mid-1300s. Also known as the Great Mortality, the Black Death was the deadliest pandemic of all time, striking Asia, Europe, and Part of Africa. The Plague caused a toll death of 25 to 200 million deaths, close to a third of the European population, in only a decade. The Black Death started from East and Central Asia with rumors of what they called the great Pestilence carving a deadly death strike along the Silk Road. (Horrox, 1994) Indeed, the Plague had another of times struck in the Asian Region, and by 1347, it was moving into Europe. In October 1347, Europe experienced a horrifying event at the Sicilian port of Messina. Twelve ships docked, and half of the sailors aboard the ships were dead, and the remaining sailors were adversely ill, covered with black boils that oozed pus and blood. The local authorities of Sicilian implemented protective measures by ordering the ships with the causalities to go away, but it was too late. In the next decade, the Plague claimed over 20 million people in the whole European Continent.

At that time, medicine was not well established; the Europeans were not ready for such sickness. An Italian poet Giovanni Boccaccio depicted that both women and men alike experienced strange swellings on either the groin or armpits and they were as big as an apple size, others size of an egg. They called this Plague boils. Furthermore, the swellings busted and oozed blood and pus while the patients experience fever, diarrhea, and after a short time of extreme pain, death followed hastily. By the time the Plague hit Sicilian, it had reached the ports of Marseille, the city of Rome, and Florence and the port of Tunis in Africa.

Chaos and panic erupted as no one at that time understood the disease, especially how it was transmitted to another person and how to treat or prevent the disease. Amidst the panic, the healthy avoided the sick, families opted to leave their loved one and flee cities to go safer places. Physicians, on the other hand, decided to use crude methods to tackle the issue, which mostly ended in death. Supernatural explanations of the disease became the talk of the day and many believed that it was some kind of punishment from God to human beings.

The Plague never really ended. Before authorities could define ways to reduce the spread hence death, the Black Death had claimed over one-third of the European population. Policies were made, which involved keeping sailors for 40 days' quarantine period at the port of arrival to determine if the Plague infected any of them. Also, those who were found with the signs they were isolated to avoid any more spread. Soon the disease become manageable although it reappeared in subsequent centuries

Chapter 1.

WHAT IS BLACK DEATH?

In the mid decades of the 1300s, a strange disease that struck the whole of Asia, northern Africa, the whole of Europe, and the Middle East, and caused a disastrous loss of both humans and animals in every city and empire the disease reached. No political, no priest, no commons, nor even science men and women understood the disease. Centuries later, the disease earned the name Black death, majorly because there was little knowledge about it.

Scientifically, after many centuries a breakthrough in understanding the disease came. The Black was described as an amalgamation of three strains; bubonic, septicemic, and pneumonic Plague. Black Death swept through the western world, causing a devastating historical loss of about 30% European population and changing history economically, socially, and religiously. A great Florentine poet Petrarch recounted that horror struck all, men, women, and the children, the rich the people, and humanity for the first time in many years seemly had an inexplicable holocaust, and there was nothing they could do. Gottfried, R. S. a German philosopher quotes Petrarch words saying, (Gottfried, 1983) He wrote to his friend, ". Oh, posterity who will not experience such abysmal woe," after watching half of the city of Florence die like animals, and, "who will look upon our testimony as a fable." He didn't believe if the future could even fathom the horror they experience, because it wrought dumbfounded havoc.

Terminologies

In the 1300s, when the disease started to bring death, a Latin name *pestilentia* was commonly used to mean epidemic. The Far North of the European Continent, the plaga which later in the fifteenth century was translated to plague in England, was put in use. According to a Norwegian historian Ole Jørgen Benedictow, the word was first used by Norway king Magnus Eriksson and Scotland king in a royal letter in late 1349. (Benedictow)The word Plague was therefore derived from a Latin word *plaga*, which meant stroke. Historians and science men up to date describe the Black Death in their different writing as mortality, '*epidamia*' or epidemic and other Pestilence.

The name Black Death has been for centuries on every memory of humans as a frightening reminder of what came close to the end of civilization. Probably, the reason why the name Black death stuck was from the common mistranslation of the Latin of *atra mors* where *atra* has both the meaning of Black and terrible. Atra Mors may have been publicized by Seneca the Younger, a Roman philanthropist, and dramatist, to refer to the disease prognostic. (Frederick, 2008) Black Death, however, was widely spoken in the 17 century as a translation of a Danish: *den sorte død* after Danish and Swish chronographers vulgarized it in three centuries of 15th, 16th, and 17th. Soon it was picked up by Germans as *der Schwarze Tod*; the French called it la *mort noire*. (Benedictow)However, before that, most European countries referred it in a Latin name *magna mortalitas*, lit meaning great death.

Background history of pandemics

Human beings have always been victims of pandemics from as early as 430 BC. In the days of hunter-gatherer, infectious and contagious diseases existed, but the human shift of lift style to agrarian revolution 10000 years ago, made it easier for pandemics to exist. As civilization grew across the world while traders forged trade routes and countries and empires waged war against each other, the spread of infectious diseases causing world pandemics became eminent. The pandemics in history to ever been recorded are as follows in descending order.

Plague of Athens

Famously named after Athens, it was the first pandemic to ever been recorded in history in 430 BC and receded in 426 BC. It greatly affected the city of Athens, hence the name Plague of Athens after its outbreak, which occurred during the Peloponnesian war (war between Spartans and Athens) that claimed the lives of about 80,000 people. Thucydides, an army general, while describing the war believed that the Plague's originated was Africa, and entered Greece through the port of Piraeus that supplied foodstuffs and other materials to Greece. (Byrne)The disease was so severe that Spartans withdrew their army to minimize their contact with the Plague upon seeing Athens people burying their dead.

The disease was highly contagious, and any contact with a sick person made you susceptible. A huge number of people died because not even medicine men were willing to risk their lives. The dead were buried in masses or cremated by relatives. People started questioning gods because they doubted if at all, they listened to their prayers. The temple dwellers, mostly refugees, were struck hardest by the disease, with the majority of them dying. They, therefore, became superstitious.

The Plague shifted the dynamics of power in Ancient Greece. The poor took over the property of the rich victims of the Plague. Those who survived became generous and even offered to look after the sick. Among the remaining citizens, those who forged their citizenship were turned into slaves, and laws were equally made stricter. It also contributed to the political weakening of the city, leading to its defeat by the Spartans. (Byrne)The causes of the disease are not known, but scientists suspect that the typhus pathogen, which causes typhoid, was responsible for the pandemic. However, sufficient scientific proof does not exist to point it out as the cause of the disease because other possibilities still exist. Ebola and Marburg virus are other possible causes of the disease. The symptoms of the Plague were high fever, bleeding and bad breath, sneezing, coughing, vomiting, insomnia, diarrhea, frequent thirst, and swelling of lymphatic nodes.

Leprosy

It was a common disease, but it massively spread across Europe in the 11th century, making it a pandemic. The bacteria Mycobacterium leprae caused it. The surge in the number of infections necessitated the building of hospitals that specifically admitted leprosy patients. At the time, people believed the disease was a curse from God. People, therefore, stigmatized leprosy patients. It still occurs to date and can result in deaths if not treated properly.

Spanish Flu

Caused by a strain of influenza virus H1N1, it occurred in the middle of world war 1, in 1918, and is recorded as the deadliest pandemic ever to occur, even in the face of modern medicine. It took away the lives of about 45 million people. In as much as it was first recorded in Europe, the USA, and Asia, its origins are not very clear. No drug or vaccine could alleviate this disease, thus worsening the pandemic. People were advised to keep a distance from one another, to wear masks, and many activities shutdown. It affected the young population adversely, and Spain recorded the highest number of deaths. It, however, faded naturally, but its effects were present in children born during that time.

HIV/AIDS

First recorded in 1981, it is a pandemic that has affected people across nations. It was first recorded in the USA, and subsequently into other parts of the world. It was at first associated with the gay population, and they were therefore stigmatized. There is still no cure for AIDS and results in the death of about a million people each year. The highest cases are in Africa, and people living with HIV/AIDS are dependent on anti-retroviral drugs to boost their immunity. Being a sexually transmitted disease, it does not spread as fast as airborne diseases.

These epidemics, among others, have marked Change the world history and order economically, religiously, and even politically. Yet even in the present, human still struggles to fight a different and new pandemic COVID 19 that is continuing to take life and destroy families and even alienating villages and city blocks.

Chapter 2.

THE ANATOMY OF A PANDEMIC - THE BLACK DEATH

The reappearance of the bubonic Plague in 1350 claimed more lives this time compared to when it first emerged. Its origins were linked to Asia, entering Europe through Sicily. When those affected by the Plague arrived at the port of Messina, their contact with other people enhanced its rapid spread across Europe. The Plague was so bad that dead bodies were left to rot in the open, and the war between England and France stopped. The British economy was not spared either since a reduction in economic activities happened. Greenland halted its fight against native North American communities.

Causes and Pathology

The Miasma Theory

In the early ages of the 1300s, people knew less about bacteria, microbiological agents, pathogens, and viruses. As a result, the majority of nations and empires believed that the disease was a divine punishment from God. For the physicians, many attributed the disease to Miasma. Consequently, a Miasma theory was believed. (Horrox) According to Horrox, an English historian who has majored in the political history of the late medieval noted that Miasma was noxious vapor pollution of the air, which contained toxic elements that were caused by putrid and rotting substances and were spread by the air or wind. Through inhaling and skin contact, scientists at that time believed Miasma could enter into a person's body. King Philip VI of France was the one who had an order for scientists to investigate and find out what was the cause of the Plague. The theory neither explained ways to cure nor prevent the Plague, although it encouraged people to be upholding hygienic ways of living to prevent rooting matter near settlements.

The Medieval Doctors

Doctors at that time had a rather obsequious responsibility of a more administrative duty because at that time there were no cures and or a comprehensive knowledge of the plague. So Doctors, kept track of victims, attended to patients and also did autopsy at times. The Local doctors saw every person regardless of their economic status and thus some got infected during their duties. To prevent contact with their patients, Charles de l'Orme, a doctor to King Louis XIII invented a doctor's suit that would protect them. (Rennie) According, Charles de l'Orme, the suit had, "a nose half a foot long, shaped like a beak, filled with perfume," to protect them from the Noxious vapor they believed caused the disease. Charles de l'Orme continued explaining in a diary that "The coat was made of Moroccan leather, together with the leggings, gloves, and boots." This was to deflect the Miasmas from head to toe. They added a black hat to identify them as doctors and also had a stick they walked around with to use it to communicate with doctors.

However, the costume was grossly flawed and caused many doctor's deaths. Many doctors who wore the costume dropped like flies and others lived in constant quarantine. The curved beak musk was stuffed with sweet herbs like camphor, mint, and cloves to combat the foul smell which came from plague patients. The beak was also punctured with holes for breathing. (Rennie)What was considered a careful way to attend to the plague patients did little to reduce the spread of the disease. Years later, thankfully, doctor's barbaric treatment methods stopped but the efforts made by doctors to save lives and bring change can never be forgotten. Today, we see the forefront doctor's working day in day out to prevent and find cures and other solutions on plague, especially the COVID 19 plague.

The New Discovery

Shortly after the 19th century, an epidemic erupted in China, Yunnan province, and in the efforts to prevent another holocaust, anti-epidemic organizations were established to combat the disease. Black Death had returned, and this time in its full strength. Reportedly, by March 1894, the Plague flared up infecting more than 400000 thousand people, and among them, only 25000 people could survive the disease. (Arrizabagala) This fueled the efforts of science men to research and find out more about the disease. Additionally, in 1870 a discovery had been made that specific bacteria caused infectious diseases. This new enlightenment, coupled with the necessity to save humankind, inspired scientists to work towards developing cures and vaccines.

The actual work to unearth the cause of the Black Death started in 1894 in Hong Kong against a backcloth of ancient medicine.

A team of bacteriologists, S. Kitasato and A. Yersin, from both Japanese and the French Government, respectively, were sent to Hong Kong. They worked in hospitals were patients affected by the Plague were, and almost immediately, they discovered a new type of Bacteria in the patient blood. Successful blood culture was done, and the bacterium was isolated. On further study, they discovered that the same bacterium was found in fleas and rodents. (Yersin) The bacterium was named after Yersin, *Yersinia pestis,* because he was the one who gave an accurate description and drew an important conclusion that rats were the principal carriers. These two men made the first breakthrough that was a real success in modern medicine. By identifying the close relationship between fleas and rodents to the Plague, it facilitated further studies and research in creating ways of transmission and dissemination, so that it would be possible to develop anti-plague measures and subsequently developing a vaccine and a cure.

The carriers- Fleas and rats

Although Yersin and his counterpart made significant breakthroughs in the bacterial studies of the Plague, there was still little knowledge of how the Plague was transmitted, how it spread, and how to fight the Plague. In 1894 a plague pandemic struck in Asia, in the areas of Hong Kong and China. The use of steamships made the Plague spread to India, Australia, Indonesia, and Madagascar. With the help of the discoveries, doctors, and scientist, this time had a basis for studying the disease. (Simpson)As a result, they find out that the Plague exhibited an identical feature of buboes like the other plagues, especially the 1346 plague pandemic. Patients developed one or two black buboes, mostly in the groin or the armpits, sometimes both. Occasionally, some patients had the buboes on their thighs, and others had on other places of the body.

Doctors found out that the buboes developed around places with a high concentration of lymph nodes. Biologically, lymph nodes act as the first line of defense against bacterial infections; that's the reason patients had swollen buboes around those areas. Therefore, this form of Plague was known as the Bubonic Plague. However, the diagnostics did not explain how the transmission of the disease occurred and how to combat the disease. In 1905, a commission was established to do more research on the Plague. (Simpson)The Indian Plague Research Commission was tasked to investigate the relation of rats and fleas and humans to the Plague. An entomologist was also recruited in the commission. Earlier in 1903 entomologist W. Glen Liston did research on fleas that were found on an infected person in the streets of Bombay. He concluded that the fleas were rat fleas that normally infest on the black rats as host animals. On further investigation on the fleas and the inhabitants of Bombay, Dr. Glen discovered that rats had a great mortality rate; hence it made it difficult for fleas to have host animals. Therefore, the fleas migrated to human. The conclusion explained the reason why there were so many dead rats in the neighborhood and streets of infected places. Particularly in Bombay, affected people increasingly complained of aggressive attack of fleas that made them find alternative places to sleep.

After two years of working on researching the connection between the fleas and humans, entomologist Glen was hired by the Indian Plague Commission. The work done at the commission was published explaining that they had proved that the Plague was a rodent disease, and the fleas and rats were vectors that transmitted the disease. (Hirst)It was understood that, in areas around the world where rodents lived in colonies, the Plague moves rapidly in the rodent's population known as the *plague focus*. In the event the *plague focus* on which live in the wild have contact with rats that inhabit the human population, an epidemic may break out.

Concerning humans and the Plague, the black rats are the major reason the pandemic was able to transmit very first. It has to be understood that these black rats loved to live in proximity to the human population. They also loved eating grains; hence they got attracted to houses, in granaries, barns, and stores.   In the 1300 century, it was known as the house rat. (Hirst)

Furthermore, because of the grains, the black rats moved to the ships, which moved from port to port. As a result, because fleas feasted on these rats, they carried that bacterium in the blood, and soon, when they lacked host animals, they moved to humans. Therefore, fleas, specifically, rat's fleas played a major role in transmitting the Plague. This finding presented a problem that the Indian Plague Commission had to be solved.

Chapter 3.

CHRONOLOGY AND TRAJECTORY OF BLACK DEATH

The importance of the Miasma theory drove people to embrace hygiene, but until then, cities were particularly very filthy. Dead animals were left unburied, human waste was disposed openly, and this attracted pests and parasites hence hastened the transmission of epidemics.

1346

The bubonic Plague was identified in Mongolia, an Asian territory. It spread to human beings through a marmot. This pandemic was very deadly and took away the lives of many dwellers of Mongolia. The dwellers then spread it to the areas around the black sea. A fight then begins between some Italian merchants and a group of Muslims. At this time, the king of Mongol, King Jani Beg, and his army have camped near the city of Tana. The death of one Muslim fled the Italian merchants to Caffa, Geonese's outpost, and Jani Beg's army went under siege where the disease infected them. The dead bodies that were dumped across city walls led to the spread of the disease in Genoese.

1347

In May, at Caffa in the Crimea region was struck severely. The survivors flee this area by the sea, as the streets become filled with dead bodies. A caftan ship that docks in Constantinople becomes infected, and nearly all the ship occupants die. In October, another ship arrives in Sicily with the crew dead. The pandemic kills almost half of the people before spreading to Messina. (Byrne) As a result of panic and despair, the inhabitants of Messina escaped their home. They spread the Plague to the rest of Italy. There the plague malady hit badly, causing a death toll of about 30% of the Italian population. The disease arrived in France in November of 1347, through a shipment that arrived in Marseille.

1348

The epidemic raged through Italy and France despite efforts put forth by the Venetian population to contain the pandemic. Neighboring cities and countries like Sicily, Greece, Bulgaria, Romania, Poland, Egypt, and Cyprus also became infected as a result, and authorities put forward policies and protective measures on docking ships. Ships that arrived at the port were thoroughly inspected, the infected ships burnt, all taverns closed, and wine that arrived from unknown locations dismissed.

In the summer of 1348, flagellants, a religious group of men, start walking half-naked, whipping themselves with lashes, begging for God's mercies. This group was first spotted in Germany. The Italian monks inspired this practice in the 11th century. The flagellants were anti-Semitics, and their practice died in 1350. Meanwhile, the disease arrived in Marseille and Normandy before one strain moves to Belgium in Tournai, while the other strain spreads to Avignon via Calais, where half of the people die. Australia and Switzerland also become infected, with the rising anti- Semitism rage. A lot of Jews were murdered because people thought they were to blame for the Plague. King Casimir III of Poland allowed the Jews to migrate to Poland, Marseilles, and Lithuania, where it was safer. The death of Princess Joan, a daughter of King Edward III, marked the arrival of the disease in London in October of this year. The city dwellers of London escape to the rural areas as the cities face food shortages. Sanitation levels of the city dropped significantly, and King Edward blamed the Plague.

1349

The worst massacres of the Jews happened on February 14, which left more than 1500 Jewish people burned while still alive. Christians also killed the Jews that tried to retaliate. In April, people escaping the Plague from England bring it to Wales, killing about 95,000 people. In July, a ship from England arriving in Norway through Bergen spreads the disease, and the ship crew dies within a week of arrival. The Plague further spreads in Denmark and Sweden. Much to the king's conviction that fasting on Fridays and walking barefoot on Sundays will please God who will then spare them from the disease, it did not work. Two brothers of the king succumbed to the sickness and spread further to Russia and the east of Greenland, halting the exploration of native north American communities by the Vikings.

1350

Scotland managed to keep itself safe from the pandemic. It, therefore, planned on taking advantage of the fact that England was adversely affected by the disease, weakening its powers, therefore a safer time to attack it. In March, Scotland soldiers became infected while at the border, thus carrying the disease back home. 30% of its population succumbed to death.

1351

By this time, the disease began to disappear naturally. Quarantine measures put in place helped curb the spread of the disease. However, the impact was devastating as half of Europe's population was affected by the pandemic, including the Jews who were killed by Christians.

1353

The disease was past now, and some changes happened in Europe. The economy revived again, given the lesser population occupying Europe then. Work was easily available, and the compensation rates were extremely good. Laws passed by Aristocrats to prevent the peasants from rising in class caused upheaval in England and France. With the passing away of the older intellectuals, new ideas sprung and led to a period of enlightenment by the youths. From then, the Plague resurfaced again in subsequent centuries, but it wasn't as fatal.

Chapter 4.

THE HYDRAHEADED MONSTER: BLACK DEATH PLAGUE

Black death plague and other Plague intrigued many researchers over different periods. Some ended up relating the Plague to mystic theories of Greeks. One particular researcher referred to the black death as a monster snake with nine heads that when you cut one head, two pop out. In Greek, the snake was killed by Hercules, and its blood was used to make poisonous arrows. In the form of a Hydra-headed monster, The Black Death plague appeared in many disguises.

Bubonic Plague. – Signs and Symptoms

Bubonic Plague is an infectious disease and one of the types of Plague caused by bacterium *Yersinia pestis.* After contact with an infected flea, it takes one to seven days for Flu-like symptoms to develop. The Plague is mainly spread by rats and infected black rat fleas and may also be spread when a victim comes into contact with the fluid of dead infected rodents, specifically house rats.

Scientifically, in this kind of Plague, the inoculated plague bacteria get transferred to the lymphatic tract going to the lymph nodes. A swelling then grows into a bubo, which mostly can be compared to the size of an egg, or perhaps an apple fruit, and is exquisitely soft. The swellings mostly developed in the leg. (World Health Organization) Patients exhibited signs where the site of the bite determined the location of a bubo. For instance, if the bite occurs on the neck, the infective bacterium will be drained lymphatic nodes at the neck area, and the bubo would develop there.

The commonly known signs of the Bubonic Plague is the enlarged and painful lymph nodes- buboes. The groin appears within three to four days after infection of the bacterium. They are commonly located at the thighs, groin, under the armpits, the neck region and the upper femoral region. (Archive Organization)Other symptoms include malaise, high fever of up to 102.2 °F (39 °C) and having chills. Other patients show signs of seizures, black dots on the body (lenticular), gangrene of places such as fingers, lips, toes, and the tip of the nose, and even coma.

Ideally, diagnosis can be made through lab tests where a culture from a patient sample is done to confirm the presence of *Y. pestis*. The samples may be blood, buboes fluid, and serum. The Plague can be prevented through sanitation, vector control, and targeted chemoprophylaxis

Septicemic Plague

In some and rare instances, a flea may take deep its proboscis directly into a vein and regurgitate the ingested blood with bits of the blockage back to the bloodstream. The amount of infection may be huge for the lymphatic system, and hence most of the bacterium will be injected into the bloodstream. In the bloodstream, rapid multiplication of the bacteria will occur, leading to a massive contraction of the Plague, and the patient health rapidly deteriorates. This Plague, also known as the primary bacteremia Plague, was and still is the most dangerous type of Black death plague since no survivors are ever there.

During a plague in the early 1910s, there were more than 100 cases where the time between infection and death was averagely fourteen hours. Locals described the disease as having a high fever in the morning and death during sun death. This Plague was the least Plague that struck in the 1300 century of the medieval period compared to Bubonic and pneumonic Plague. Benedictow depicts that (Benedictow) the Plague was the most dangerous as it did not leave any external signs and only attacked the spirit of life in the heart. The death occurred even before the buboes developed.

In this Plague, bacterial endotoxins cause multiple tiny blood clots all over the body which eventually causes the death of body and blood tissues due to lack of blood circulation and perfusion. (Wobeser) Professor Gary Wobeser in the Department of Veterinary Pathology (Western College of Veterinary Medicine, Canada) explains in his book that, the bacteria disseminate intravascular coagulation, which reduces the ability of the body to clot and hence lead to uncontrolled bleeding. As a result, the excessive un-clotted blood bleeds profusely under the skin and in other body organs, and thus, black and red parches occur on the patient body. Sometimes, the patient may cough up and vomit blood.

Septicemic Plague is particularly caused by more than a flea bite. There are cases even though rare; people got infected by the Plague without being bitten by a flea. The Plague can be transmitted horizontally or directly. (Wobeser)Direct transmission occurs direct bite of an infected house rat flea or sometimes close physical contact with the infected. Whereas, horizontal occurs when the disease gets transmitted from one person to another regardless of their blood relations.

Pneumonic Plague

Following an initial infection of Bubonic Plague, a severe lung infection caused by the *Y. pestis* bacteria may occur. The distinguishing factor between the different plagues it's the location of the Plague. For Pneumonic Plague the *Y. pestis* bacteria attack the lungs. (World Health Organization)The Plague is caused by the breathing of aerosolized bacteria droplets that come from a plague-infected person or rodent. The Plague also can be a secondary infection, specifically when Septicemic Plague moves to the lungs. This is on the type of Plague that occurred in Black Death.

Patients suffering from this Plague exhibited signs like extreme hemoptysis- coughing of blood-, having high fever, and developing shortness of breath rapidly. (Archive Organization) Other signs include bloody sputum, chest pain, nausea, and coughing. The signs may continue for three to four days, and the patient will succumb to death.

Chapter 5.

HISTORIC CHANGES CAUSED BY BLACK DEATH

Population reintegrate

The mortality rate of Black that occurred in the 14th century was extremely devastating compared to any other plague outbreaks before and after the 14th century caused by Y.Pestis bacterium. The Plague wiped out an estimated population of 75 to 200 million people both in Europe and Asia. Historians like Ole Benedictow estimate that because the disease spread so fast that no doctors or authority could have the chance to control, it killed almost 60% of the European population. (Benedictow)For instance, within four months after the disease struck Port Florence city, tax records of the old city suggest more than 75% of the population at that time perished in 1348. By 1850, half of Germans were reduced to dust as the Plague wiped many settlements leaving most towns and cities with no human alive.

On account of the Papacy physician Raimundo Chalmel de Vinario, who was in charge of Avignon Papacy's health, he noted his 1382 Treatise *On Epidemics*, that there was a decrease in mortality of the Plague as years passed. In the Treatise, he notes that the first outbreak of 1346-47 infected 75% of the population in Europe and almost half, the number died. (Byrne , Joseph Patrick) In the next outbreak of 1362, 50% of the population got infected, but only a few got killed. By the time it reached 1382, one in ten people had died of the Plague.

Social

Socially, Black death prompted a new way of living that was not there before. Humans, especially in the city of Florence, dwelled more on the productivity of their lives rather than spirituality. Its argued that the devastation of the city of Florence pushed the citizen to transcend to modernity by changing how they socially, educationally, and economically did their things as the church as unable to offer solutions against the Black Death. As a result, this led to Renaissances- a transition period from middle ages to modernity in Europe occurring between 14th to 16th centuries. There is no clear understanding of how Renaissances started. Still, many theories relate to factors like civic and social peculiarities of Florence, the great tyranny of the family of Medici, together with its political structure. Also, the migration of Greeks to Italy contributed to the complexity of the Renaissances. The spirit of Renaissances then spread to many other cities and countries; soon it reached all of Europe.

Economic

As a result of the huge loss of populations because of the plague pandemic, labor shortage increased rapidly, and therefore wages soared. Trading faced huge inflation as goods were scarce, and those supplied fetched high demand. In housing, landlords were forced to reduce sometimes remove rent in exchange for getting labor.

Persecutions

A new wave of enthusiasm and fanaticism bloomed amid the ravaging Black Death. Various groups, including leapers, Jews, friars, foreigner, and beggars, were targeted by a group of misguided Europeans who blamed them for the pandemic. At that time, medicine and science had no explanation of what was happening, even empire administration, and perhaps the church did not completely understand the Plague. Hence some physicians order by King Philip VI concluded on Miasma theory. They believed that it comes from some astrological forces and poisoning. (David) As a result, some Europeans believed the Jews had something to do with poisoning the wells, which would be the possible cause for the Plague. Hence, Jews became a target in the 1340s, and multiple Jews communities suffered persecutions.

In 1349, a total of over 2000 Jews were murdered in Strasbourg, and this was only the beginning. Many other cities followed. In the same year on August Jewish communities in Mainz and Cologne were burnt and destroyed, not leaving any soul alive. (Jewish History Organization) By the early 1350s, 210 Jewish communities had been destroyed. Many believed the Plague was a punishment from God for the sins they had committed.

Chapter 6.

REOCCURRENCE

The Second Plague.

Black Death return severally in Europe and Asia, with the same intensity as the first major Plague. In 1361-63 the Plague reoccurred in Italy. The cities of Venice, Florence, Pisa and Pistoia, were adversely affected as *pesta Secunda* swept a 5th of the Italian population. (White) This recurrence was the first one after the major pandemic that happened in the decade of 1340. In Italy alone there were 22 outbreaks of the Plague up to the 15th century from 1346. Francesco Petrarca, an Italian poet, wrote to humanists Giovanni Boccaccio during the Italian Renaissances complaining of how wrong people though the Plague was a one-time unprecedented disaster in Europe, yet, it seemed that it was only the beginning of mourning and suffering for years.

In 1400 century, believers were celebrating the Jubilee Year in Rome, before the Plague struck the city of Rome and the neighboring one with much intensity killing half of the population of Pistoia. In Rome, the Plague killed 600 people daily. In the same century, around 1478- 1482, the Plague struck the city of Florence, killing 300000 people in eight years. (White)According to Luca Landucci (1436–1516), he describes the deaths in the city of Florence saying " the citizens of Florence were in a sorry plight. All of them lived in despair, and no one wanted to work. The poor creatures could not procure silk or wool so that all classes suffered."

However, several different sources confirm that the Plague also recurred in Asia and Sub- Haran Africa. The Plague ravaged the Islamic nations in the middle east virtually every year from 1500to 1800. (White)In northern Africa 1620-1621, the Algerians were struck by the Plague, and 50000 people died. It returned in 1654-69 and 1740-42. In the horn of Africa, the Plague killed so many Egyptians for over 150 years. Cairo to be specifically suffered over fifty plague outbreaks until the 18th century when the Plague disappeared.

The Third Plague

In the 18 century, the Plague struck Asian China and India. From 1855 through 1859 an approximate of 10 million inhabitants died in India alone. As a result, commissions like the Indian Plague commission was established leading to the breakthrough of discovering the *Yersinia pestis*

Disappearances of the Plague

Although the 18th and 19th plague outbreaks were very severe, it also marked a significant drop in the number of outbreaks and infections around the world. Even though scientists had now begun to understand the Plague, the pandemic progressively ceased across the European Continent and Asia. (Appleby) For reasons not understood, the Plague was last recorded in Europe during that century in 1679, 13 years after the London Great Fire. Some conclude and believe that the fire ceased another outbreak of the Plague. Probably, it is because, after the fire, all houses were constructed with bricks.

However, the patterns of the decrease continued across the whole of Europe. Possible explanations spurred between science and evolution. Some concluded that humans might have developed immunity against the disease; others suggested that the improvement in the level of cleanliness also had contributed. (Appleby) Others maintained that the rats' species changed and the brown rat now became dominant, while some sources insisted that the improvement of the quarantine method also contributed to the disappearance. Also, revolutionaries suggested that the evolution process may not have favored the bacterium strain causing the Plague. Nevertheless, all the thought and considered hypothesis may have contributed to the disappearance even though a conclusive reason was not determined.

Fatality rate.

Using the modern case study of the Plague, and after the introduction of antibiotics, the fatality rate of the bubonic Plague is 11%. (Centers for Disease Control (CDC) ()

CONCLUSION

The Black Death pandemic struck in the mid-1300s. Also known as the Great Mortality, the Black Death was the deadliest pandemic of all time, striking Asia, Europe, and Part of Africa. The Plague caused a toll death of 25 to 200 million deaths, close to a third of the European population, in only a decade. The Black Death started from East and Central Asia with rumors of what they called the great Pestilence carving a deadly death strike along the Silk Road. (Horrox, 1994) Indeed, the Plague had another of times struck in the Asian Region, and by 1347, it was moving into Europe. In October 1347, Europe experienced a horrifying event at the Sicilian port of Messina. Twelve ships docked, and half of the sailors aboard the ships were dead, and the remaining sailors were adversely ill, covered with black boils that oozed pus and blood. The plague only started at a port but ended with enormous death tolls around the whole world.

Today the world faces another plague and as everyone is hustling through the day, with different agendas and goals, the plague continues to kill humans, destroying families and nations and changing history.

WORKS CITED

Jewish History Organization. <u>History of Jews in 1340-1350</u>. 12 Novemeber 2007. <jewishhistory.org.il>.

Appleby, Andrew B. ""The Disappearance of Plague: A Continuing Puzzle"." <u>The Economic History Review,</u> 6 May 1980: 161–173, doi:10.1111/j.1468-0289.1980.tb01821.

Archive Organization . <u>Plague</u> . 03 April 2012. <web.archive.org >.

Arrizabagala, Jon. "Plague and epidemics". In Bjork, Robert Ed." <u>The Oxford Dictionary of the Middle Ages.</u> (2010): 50-78.

Benedictow, Ole L. <u>The Black Death, 1346-1353: The Complete History</u>. Woodbridge England: Boydell Press, 2004.

Byrne , Joseph Patrick . "" (Magister Riamundus; Chalmelli: Chalin;d after 1382) Vinario, Raimundo Chalmel de ." <u>Encyclopedia of the Black Death</u> (2012): p 352-55.

Byrne, Joseph Patrick. ""Caffa (Kaffa, Fyodosia), Ukraine"." <u>Encyclopedia of the Black Death</u> (2010): p 64-67.

Centers for Disease Control (CDC) (. ""Madagascar Wrestles With Worst Outbreak of Plague in Half a Century." <u>Wall Street Journal.</u> (November 2014): 34-56.

David, Nirenburg. <u>Communities of Violence</u> . Princeton: Princeton University Press , 1998.

Frederick, Ahl. <u>Two Faces of Oedipus</u>. Ithaca, Newyork: Cornell Univ. Press, 2008.

Gottfried, Robert S. <u>The Black Dath : Natural and Human Disaster</u>

in Mediaval Europe. Newyork : The Free Press , 1983.

Hirst, Fabian L. The Conquest of Plague. New York: Oxford University Press, 1953.

Horrox, Rosemary. The Black Death. England: Oxford Press , 1994.

Rennie, Daniel. Inside The Terrifying But Necessary Job Of A Medieval Plague Doctor. 16 January 2019. <https://allthatsinteresting.com/plague-doctors>.

Simpson, W.J. A Treatise On Plague. London: Cambridge University Press , 1905 .

White, Arthur. "The Four Horsemen". Plague and Pleasure: The Renaissance World of Pius II. Washington D.C.: : Catholic University of America Press., 2014.

Wobeser, Gary A. Esssentials of disease in Wild Animals. Oxford : Blackwell Publishing , 2006.

World Health Organization. Facts sheets: Plague . 31 October 2017. <www.who.int/en/news-room/fact-sheets/details/ plague>.

Yersin, Alexandre. " "La peste bubonique a Hong-Kong"." Annales de l'Institut Pasteur: Journal de microbiologie. (1894): (9):667-69.

YOUR FREE EBOOKS FROM HISTORY HOUSE!

Hello Dear History Readers!

I'm Alexander MacDonald and I created History House.

As a way of saying **Thank You** for reading our book series from History House, we're offering you a free e-Book copy every **weekend!**

Happy Reading ☺

>> Click Here <<

>> To Get Your FREE eBook <<

OTHER BOOKS BY HISTORY HOUSE:

The Spanish Flu of 1918 The Story of a Forgotten Pandemic

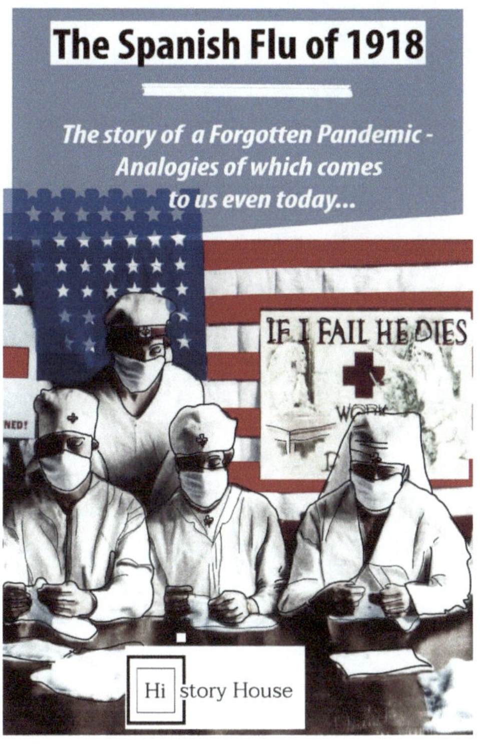

US Kindle, UK Kindle, CA Kindle, AU Kindle * Available on all kindle markets

The Life of Anne Frank Fascinate Journey from the early years to an end

US Kindle, UK Kindle, CA Kindle, AU Kindle
* Available on all kindle markets

The Life of Sir Winston Churchill: Fascinate Journey - From The Early Years to an End

US Kindle, UK Kindle, CA Kindle, AU Kindle * Available on all kindle markets

The Life of Albert Einstein: Fascinate Journey - From the early years to an end

US Kindle, UK Kindle, CA Kindle, AU Kindle * Available on all kindle markets

YOUR REVIEW IS IMPORTANT TO US ☺

If you enjoyed this book, found it useful or otherwise, then we would really appreciate it if you would post a short review on Amazon.

We do read all the reviews personally so that we can continually write what people are wanting.

If you'd like to leave a review, then please visit the link below on Amazon:

Click Here to Leave a Review

Thank you for your support!